Awakened Eating

*A 6 week Guide to Transforming
Your Relationship With Food*

BETHANY ORRICK

BALBOA.PRESS
A DIVISION OF HAY HOUSE

Copyright © 2024 Bethany Orrick.

All rights reserved. No part of this book may be used or reproduced by any means, graphic, electronic, or mechanical, including photocopying, recording, taping or by any information storage retrieval system without the written permission of the author except in the case of brief quotations embodied in critical articles and reviews.

Balboa Press books may be ordered through booksellers or by contacting:

Balboa Press
A Division of Hay House
1663 Liberty Drive
Bloomington, IN 47403
www.balboapress.com
844-682-1282

Because of the dynamic nature of the Internet, any web addresses or links contained in this book may have changed since publication and may no longer be valid. The views expressed in this work are solely those of the author and do not necessarily reflect the views of the publisher, and the publisher hereby disclaims any responsibility for them.

The author of this book does not dispense medical advice or prescribe the use of any technique as a form of treatment for physical, emotional, or medical problems without the advice of a physician, either directly or indirectly. The intent of the author is only to offer information of a general nature to help you in your quest for emotional and spiritual well-being. In the event you use any of the information in this book for yourself, which is your constitutional right, the author and the publisher assume no responsibility for your actions.

Any people depicted in stock imagery provided by Getty Images are models, and such images are being used for illustrative purposes only. Certain stock imagery © Getty Images.

Print information available on the last page.

ISBN: 979-8-7652-5631-2 (sc)
ISBN: 979-8-7652-5632-9 (e)

Balboa Press rev. date: 10/11/2024

For Sam, my love and constant companion on this journey of discovery and growth. Thank you for walking beside me as we awaken to a new way of living and eating together.

CONTENTS

Awakened Eating 1

Listening to My Body 3

Body Scan Meditation 10

My Journey to Intermittent Fasting 15

Why Intermittent Fasting Works 19

Activation of Fat Burning 21

Slowing Down My Eating 36

Appreciating My Food 46

Mindful Eating Practice 53

Engaging All My Senses 54

Becoming Non-Judgmental 62

Closing Meditation: Embracing Inner Strength for Healthy
Choices 74

Final Thoughts 77

AWAKENED EATING

Welcome to Awakened Eating. Here you will transition to new healthy habits of enlightened eating, a practice that not only benefits your physical health but also nourishes your soul.

You will be guided through the principles of awakened eating, meditation exercises, questions for reflection, and opportunities to deepen your spiritual connection with food.

This experience has been designed to explain and help you:

- Understand the principles of Awakened Eating.
- Practice meditation techniques to enhance mindfulness.
- Reflect on personal eating habits and their emotional and spiritual implications.
- Cultivate a deeper connection with food and its source.

Understanding Awakened Eating

Awakened Eating is the practice of paying full attention to the experience of eating and drinking, both inside and outside the body. It involves noticing the colors, smells, textures, flavors, temperatures, and even the sounds of our food. It's also about recognizing our body's hunger and satiety signals.

Principles of Awakened Eating:

Listen to Your Body: Recognize hunger and fullness cues.

Slow Down: Take your time to eat and savor each bite.

Appreciate Your Food: Acknowledge the journey of your food from farm to table.

Engage All Senses: Use your senses to fully experience your food.

Non-Judgment: Be aware of and let go of any judgmental thoughts about food or eating habits.

LISTENING TO MY BODY

Listening to my body was not something I grew up knowing how to do. For years, I struggled with emotional eating, turning to food when I was stressed, bored, or sad. I ate quickly, barely tasting my food, and often found myself uncomfortably full without realizing it until it was too late. My relationship with food felt out of control, and I knew something had to change.

It wasn't until I developed awakened eating and learned to listen to my body that things started to shift. One day, after a particularly stressful morning at work, I found myself reaching for a snack out of habit. But this time, I paused. I remembered the concept of hunger and fullness cues and asked myself: "Am I really hungry, or am I just stressed?"

I took a moment to reflect on my physical sensations. My stomach wasn't growling, and I didn't feel lightheaded or low on energy. In fact, I was comfortably full from breakfast just a few hours earlier. The realization hit me—I wasn't hungry at all. I was just looking for comfort in food. This was my first step toward tuning into my body's signals.

That evening, I decided to put the practice into action with dinner. I rated my hunger before eating, realizing I was at a solid "4" on the hunger scale—hungry but not ravenous. I made a conscious effort to eat slowly, putting my fork down between bites and savoring the flavors of my meal. About halfway through, I checked in with myself: "Am I still hungry?" I noticed I was starting to feel full, but I still had some food left on my plate. Normally, I would have finished it all without thinking twice, but this time, I stopped.

After the meal, I reflected on how I felt. I wasn't stuffed or uncomfortable for once. Instead, I felt satisfied, both physically and emotionally. It was a small but significant victory.

Over the next few weeks, I made it a habit to practice mindful eating at least once a day. I kept a hunger and fullness journal, jotting down my physical and emotional states before and after meals. At first, it was hard to remember to pause and check in with myself. But the more I practiced, the more natural it became. I started to notice patterns—like how I would crave certain foods when I was tired or anxious. Rather than denying myself, I learned to honor those cravings in moderation, savoring a piece of chocolate when I wanted it without guilt or overindulgence.

One of the most profound changes came during a particularly busy day at work. I had skipped lunch because of back-to-back meetings, and by the time I got home, I was starving—a solid "2" on the hunger scale. In the past, I would have torn into a bag of chips and eaten until I was stuffed, barely paying attention to what I was doing. But this time, I paused, took a few deep breaths, and prepared a balanced meal. I ate slowly, checking in with myself every few bites. Even though I was famished, I didn't rush. By the end of the meal, I felt comfortably full, not overly

AWAKENED EATING

stuffed, and I was proud of myself for listening to my body rather than eating out of sheer desperation.

Mindful eating has transformed my relationship with food. I no longer eat on autopilot or use food as a way to cope with my emotions. Instead, I approach meals with intention, paying attention to my body's signals and respecting its needs. It's not always easy, and there are still days when I slip into old habits. But each time I return to the practice, I feel more connected to myself and more in tune with what my body truly needs.

It's a journey, and I'm still learning. But by listening to my body, I've found a sense of balance and peace with food that I never thought possible.

Week 1 Listening to Your Body

Listening to your body involves tuning into the signals it sends regarding hunger, fullness, and overall well-being.

Here are some practical steps to help you get started:

Steps to Listen to Your Body

Hunger Signals and Physical Sensations:

- Stomach growling
- Feeling lightheaded
- low energy.

Mental Signs:

- Difficulty concentrating
- Irritability

Fullness Signals:

- Stomach feels comfortably full, not bloated.
- Loss of interest in food, feeling satisfied.

Rate Your Hunger

Before eating, take a moment to assess your hunger on a scale from 1 to 10:

1-2: Starving, very hungry.

3-4: Hungry, ready to eat.

5-6: Comfortable, not hungry but not full.

7-8: Full, but not overly so.

9-10: Uncomfortably full, very stuffed.

Chew Thoroughly: Take time to chew each bite thoroughly, at least 20-30 times, savoring the flavors and textures, before swallowing.

Pause Between Bites: Put your utensils down between bites to give your body time to signal fullness.

Engage Your Senses: Pay attention to the taste, smell, and appearance of your food.

Check In Mid-Meal

Halfway through your meal, pause and assess your hunger and fullness levels again.

Ask yourself:

- Am I still hungry?
- How does my stomach feel?

Honor Your Cravings

Recognize when you're craving certain foods and understand why. Cravings can sometimes indicate nutritional needs or emotional states. Allow yourself to enjoy the foods you crave in moderation. Slowly savor your first 3 bites of what you crave, then check yourself. Our taste buds give us our most intense flavors in our first 3 bites. After that the flavors start to dull in taste. Check yourself. Are you still enjoying the taste?

Reflect After Eating

After finishing your meal, take a moment to reflect on how you feel:

- Are you comfortably full or overly stuffed?
- Do you feel satisfied and content?

Practice Regularly Listening to your body is a skill that improves with practice. Regularly checking in with yourself before, during, and after meals will help you become more attuned to your body's signals.

Exercises for Week 1

Hunger and Fullness Journal

Keep a journal for a week to track your hunger and fullness levels before and after each meal.

- Note what you ate
- Your hunger level before eating
- Your fullness level after eating, and any emotions you experienced

Mindful Eating Practice

Choose one meal per day to practice Awakened Eating:

Set the Table: Create a pleasant eating environment without distractions.

Take Your Time: Eat slowly, focusing on each bite, chew at least 15 times.

Check In: Pause midway to assess your hunger and fullness levels.

Reflect: After the meal, take a moment to reflect on the experience.

Listening to your body is a crucial aspect of mindful eating. By tuning into your hunger and fullness cues, eating mindfully, and reflecting on your eating experiences, you can develop a healthier, more intuitive relationship with food. With practice, you'll find it easier to honor your body's needs and enjoy a more fulfilling and balanced approach to eating.

BODY SCAN MEDITATION

In the stillness of the moment, we turn our attention inward, embarking on a journey through the body, starting from the front of the feet and gradually moving upward. This practice is a mindful exploration of physical sensations, a gentle yet profound way to connect with our bodies, and to cultivate awareness of the present moment. As you settle into a comfortable position, either seated or lying down, allow yourself to release any tension or thoughts that may be occupying your mind. Breathe deeply, feeling the rise and fall of your chest, and let your breath guide you through this body scan meditation.

Bring your attention to the front of your feet, where they connect with the ground or the surface beneath you. Notice the sensations here—the contact with the floor, the texture of your socks or shoes, the temperature of the air against your skin. Perhaps you feel a sense of grounding, as if your feet are roots connecting you to the earth. Take a moment to appreciate this connection, to feel the stability and support that your feet provide.

Slowly shift your focus to your toes. Wiggle them slightly if you can, or simply notice their presence. Feel the individual toes, from the big toe to the smallest one. Notice any sensations—tingling,

AWAKENED EATING

warmth, or coolness. Observe the space between your toes, the flexibility of each joint. If there is any tension or discomfort, acknowledge it without judgment. Imagine your breath flowing into your toes, softening and relaxing them with each exhale.

As you continue to breathe deeply, move your awareness up to your ankles. These joints bear the weight of your body and allow for movement and flexibility. Notice the sensations here—perhaps a slight stretch or a feeling of looseness. Rotate your ankles gently if it feels comfortable, and as you do, observe how this movement affects the rest of your feet. Allow your breath to soothe any tightness, bringing a sense of ease to this area.

With each breath, let your awareness travel up to your shins and calves. These muscles and bones work in harmony to support your every step. Notice the texture of your skin, the sensation of your clothing against these areas. Feel the strength of your calves, the way they hold you up and propel you forward. If there is any tension, imagine it dissolving with each exhale, replaced by a sense of lightness and relaxation.

Now bring your focus to your knees, those remarkable joints that allow for such a wide range of movement. Notice the bend of your knees, the position they are in, and any sensations that arise— whether it's a feeling of stability, warmth, or even discomfort. Acknowledge your knees with gratitude, for they play a crucial role in your ability to walk, run, and move. Breathe into any areas of tightness, allowing your breath to bring a sense of ease.

As your attention moves upward to your thighs, feel the strength of these large muscles. Notice the weight of your legs pressing down, the contact with the surface beneath you. Your thighs are powerful, carrying you through your day with endurance. Take a moment to appreciate this power, to recognize the effort these muscles exert. If there is any tightness or heaviness, imagine your breath gently massaging the muscles, bringing relaxation and release.

Now bring your awareness to your hips and pelvis, the center of your body's movement and balance. Notice how your hips are positioned, the alignment of your pelvis. Feel the connection between your hips and the ground, how they support the upper body. This area is often a storehouse for tension or emotions, so take a moment to check in with any sensations here. Breathe deeply into your hips, imagining the breath flowing into any areas of tightness or discomfort, allowing them to soften and release.

As you continue to breathe deeply and evenly, shift your focus to your abdomen. This is the core of your body, home to vital organs and the center of your breath. Notice the rise and fall of your belly with each breath, the expansion and contraction. Feel the warmth of your body, the subtle movements that occur with every inhalation and exhalation. If there is any tension, allow your breath to flow into your abdomen, bringing a sense of lightness and relaxation.

Now bring your attention to your chest, where your heart beats steadily, pumping life through your body. Feel the rhythm of your heartbeat, the expansion of your chest with each breath. Notice the sensations here—the warmth, the movement, the energy. Take a moment to connect with your heart, the center of love and compassion within you. Breathe deeply, allowing your heart to soften and open, filling your chest with a sense of peace and contentment.

AWAKENED EATING

As your awareness moves upward, focus on your shoulders and neck. These areas often carry the weight of the world, storing tension and stress. Notice how your shoulders are positioned, the sensations in your neck. If there is any tightness, imagine your breath flowing into these areas, softening and relaxing them. Feel your shoulders gently releasing, your neck lengthening and relaxing. Allow the breath to bring a sense of ease and lightness.

Now shift your focus to your arms, from your shoulders down to your hands. Notice the sensations in your upper arms, your elbows, your forearms. Feel the weight of your arms, the way they rest against your body or the surface beneath you. Bring your awareness to your hands, the fingers, the palms. These are the tools with which you interact with the world, creating, touching, holding. Take a moment to appreciate the versatility and strength of your hands. Breathe into any areas of tension, allowing your arms and hands to relax fully.

Finally, bring your attention to your head and face. Notice the position of your head, the sensations in your scalp. Feel the softness of your forehead, the space around your eyes, the ease in your jaw. These areas often hold subtle tension, so take a moment to check in with them. Breathe deeply, imagining your breath flowing into your face, softening any tightness, smoothing out any creases. Allow your entire head to relax, your face to soften, your mind to become clear and calm.

As you complete this body scan, take a moment to notice how your body feels as a whole. From the front of your feet up to the crown of your head, you have brought your awareness to every part of your body, cultivating a deep sense of presence and relaxation. Breathe deeply, feeling the connection between your breath and your body, the unity of mind and body. When you are ready, gently bring your awareness back to the room, to the space around you. Open your eyes if they were closed, and take a moment to appreciate the calm and peace you have cultivated through this practice. Carry this sense of mindfulness with you as you move forward into your day, grounded and centered in the present moment.

MY JOURNEY TO INTERMITTENT FASTING

For years, I struggled with maintaining a consistent weight and energy level. Like many, I tried various diets—low carb, calorie counting, meal prepping—but none seemed to offer lasting results. Every time I restricted my eating, I felt deprived, and the moment I gave myself some freedom, the weight would come back. It was an exhausting cycle. Then, I came across intermittent fasting (IF), and while I was skeptical at first, it has been a game changer for me in ways I hadn't anticipated.

I first heard about intermittent fasting from a friend who was raving about how it had transformed not just her body, but her relationship with food. She explained how it wasn't about cutting out any specific foods or obsessively watching calories, but simply eating during a designated window and fasting the rest of the time. I decided to give it a try, choosing a 16:8 method—16 hours of fasting followed by an 8-hour eating window.

At first, the idea of not eating breakfast was daunting. I had always been told that breakfast was the most important meal of the day, and skipping it felt unnatural. But I powered through, telling myself it was only for a week. The first few days were challenging—I felt hungry in the mornings, and I had moments where I'd catch myself instinctively reaching for a snack out of habit, not hunger. But surprisingly, by the third day, something started to shift.

I began to notice that my hunger wasn't as intense as I had imagined. My energy remained steady throughout the morning, and by the time I had my first meal at noon, I was eating mindfully, savoring each bite rather than rushing through my food. For the first time in years, I felt in control of my hunger instead of letting it control me.

What struck me most was how quickly my body seemed to adapt. By the second week, I wasn't even thinking about food during the fasting window. My meals became more deliberate and enjoyable, and I started to notice changes in my body. My clothes fit a little looser, and I could tell I was losing fat, particularly around my midsection, where I had always struggled. It made sense once I understood the science behind intermittent fasting—how the body switches from burning glucose to burning fat once glycogen stores are depleted during fasting. I was finally accessing that stored fat for energy, something no other diet had helped me achieve in such a sustainable way.

The most surprising part of this journey was how much more in tune I became with my body. I learned to recognize the difference between true hunger and emotional cravings. Instead of snacking out of boredom or stress, I began listening to my body's actual cues. On days when I was hungrier earlier in my eating window, I honored that hunger without guilt, trusting that my body would regulate itself. Intermittent fasting wasn't just about losing weight for me—it was about developing a healthier, more intuitive relationship with food.

As I continued, I noticed other unexpected benefits. My energy levels were more consistent throughout the day. I no longer experienced that mid-afternoon crash that would leave me sluggish and reaching for sugary snacks. I even found that my mental clarity improved. I later learned that this is likely due to the increased production of brain-derived neurotrophic factor (BDNF) that happens during fasting. My mind felt sharper, and I was more focused at work than I had been in years.

Another powerful aspect of intermittent fasting for me was the simplicity. I wasn't constantly thinking about food or planning complex meals. I ate during my window, and outside of that, food didn't occupy so much of my mind. It felt freeing. There was no longer the stress of constantly counting calories or eliminating entire food groups. Instead, I could enjoy the foods I loved, but within a structure that supported my goals.

Perhaps the most profound benefit came in the form of my overall health. Not only did I lose weight, but my blood sugar levels stabilized, and I noticed improvements in my digestion and sleep. My body felt more resilient and balanced. Learning that fasting triggers autophagy—the process where cells clean out old or damaged parts—helped me understand why I felt so rejuvenated. I wasn't just burning fat; I was giving my body time to repair and renew itself from the inside out.

Looking back, intermittent fasting was the first method that truly resonated with my lifestyle. It was sustainable in the long term, didn't require expensive supplements or complicated rules, and gave me the freedom to live my life without constantly stressing over food. It wasn't a quick fix—it was a lifestyle change, one that helped me not only reach my health goals but sustain them.

BETHANY ORRICK

Intermittent fasting has become more than a tool for weight management for me. It's a way to honor my body's natural rhythms, improve my overall well-being, and feel empowered in my health journey. It taught me that sometimes less is more—by simply giving my body the space and time it needs to heal, I unlocked benefits far beyond what I had imagined.

WHY INTERMITTENT FASTING WORKS

Intermittent fasting (IF) has gained significant popularity in recent years as a method for weight management and overall health improvement. Its appeal lies not only in its simplicity but in its scientifically backed mechanisms that align with our body's natural rhythms. In this chapter, we will explore the reasons why intermittent fasting works, diving into the physiological, hormonal, and behavioral factors that make it an effective approach to health and wellness.

Hormonal Regulation and Insulin Sensitivity

At the heart of why intermittent fasting works is its effect on the body's hormones, particularly insulin. Insulin is the hormone responsible for regulating blood sugar levels by facilitating the storage of glucose in cells. When we eat frequently, especially high-carbohydrate meals, our insulin levels spike to manage the incoming glucose. If this cycle continues with little rest, it can lead to insulin resistance—a condition where cells become less responsive to insulin, resulting in higher blood sugar levels, fat storage, and eventually, diseases like type 2 diabetes.

Intermittent fasting helps break this cycle by giving the body periods of time when insulin levels remain low. During the fasting window, the body's insulin sensitivity improves, meaning cells become more efficient at processing glucose when you do eat. This is a key factor in why intermittent fasting promotes weight loss and prevents insulin resistance. With lower insulin levels, the body is encouraged to use stored fat as a source of energy, leading to fat loss over time.

ACTIVATION OF FAT BURNING

One of the most compelling aspects of intermittent fasting is its ability to switch the body from a glucose-burning state to a fat-burning state. When food is unavailable for an extended period, the body taps into its glycogen stores (stored glucose) in the liver for energy. Once glycogen stores are depleted, the body switches to using fat as its primary energy source through a process called lipolysis.

This metabolic shift typically occurs after 12-16 hours of fasting, depending on individual metabolism and activity levels. As the body burns fat for fuel, weight loss naturally follows. Additionally, this process may contribute to a reduction in abdominal fat, which is particularly harmful to health.

Cellular Cleansing and Longevity

Intermittent fasting does more than just promote fat loss. One of its most powerful benefits is its ability to trigger autophagy, a process where cells break down and remove old or damaged components. This cellular "clean-up" process is crucial for maintaining healthy cell function, reducing inflammation, and preventing the accumulation of harmful substances that can lead to disease, including cancer and neurodegenerative disorders like Alzheimer's.

During fasting, the body's energy is not spent on digestion, allowing it to focus on repairing and regenerating cells. Autophagy is often referred to as the body's natural detoxification system, and it has been linked to increased longevity and improved health outcomes. By giving your body regular periods of fasting, you essentially activate this self-healing mechanism, helping to protect against aging and illness.

Enhanced Human Growth Hormone (HGH) Production

Another reason intermittent fasting works so well is its ability to stimulate the production of human growth hormone (HGH). HGH plays a significant role in fat metabolism, muscle building, and overall cell regeneration. Studies have shown that fasting can increase HGH levels by up to 5-fold, making it an effective tool for those looking to build lean muscle while burning fat.

Higher HGH levels are also associated with improved recovery, faster healing, and increased muscle mass retention during weight loss. This hormonal shift is part of what makes intermittent fasting an attractive option for athletes or anyone seeking to improve body composition.

Improved Brain Health and Cognitive Function

Intermittent fasting has positive effects on brain health, primarily through the increase of brain-derived neurotrophic factor (BDNF). BDNF is a protein that supports the growth, survival, and differentiation of neurons, helping improve memory, learning, and cognitive function. Fasting triggers the production of BDNF, which promotes brain plasticity and resilience.

Additionally, intermittent fasting has been shown to reduce oxidative stress and inflammation, both of which are linked to neurodegenerative diseases. The ketogenic state (where the body uses ketones, derived from fat, for fuel) produced by fasting also supports brain health by providing a more efficient and stable energy source than glucose.

Simplicity and Behavioral Benefits

From a practical standpoint, intermittent fasting works because it simplifies eating. Rather than worrying about meal planning or calorie counting throughout the day, you have designated periods for eating and fasting. This structure naturally reduces overeating and promotes mindfulness around food.

Moreover, intermittent fasting has been shown to improve appetite regulation. The body adapts to fasting by reducing hunger hormone levels like ghrelin, meaning that over time, people often feel less hungry during fasting periods. This can lead to a more sustainable approach to weight management, as the cravings and constant need to snack decrease.

Metabolic Flexibility

Metabolic flexibility refers to the body's ability to efficiently switch between using carbohydrates and fats for energy. Intermittent fasting trains the body to be more metabolically flexible by regularly depleting glycogen stores and encouraging fat utilization. This improves overall energy efficiency and reduces reliance on frequent carbohydrate intake to maintain energy levels.

As a result, many people find that they have more stable energy throughout the day and experience fewer energy crashes, particularly during the fasting window.

Sustainability and Long-Term Benefits

Unlike many traditional diets that focus on restricting specific food groups or obsessively counting calories, intermittent fasting emphasizes timing rather than what you eat. This makes it a more sustainable long-term approach for many people, as it doesn't require significant changes to your diet. You can still enjoy the foods you love, just within a set window of time.

The long-term benefits of intermittent fasting extend beyond weight loss. Improved metabolic health, better blood sugar control, lower inflammation levels, and enhanced cognitive function are all sustainable outcomes. These benefits, coupled with the fact that intermittent fasting requires no expensive supplements or complicated meal plans, make it an accessible and practical option for a wide range of people.

Intermittent fasting works because it aligns with the body's natural processes. By regulating insulin levels, promoting fat

AWAKENED EATING

burning, enhancing cellular repair, and improving hormonal balance, it optimizes our physiology for health and longevity. Additionally, its simplicity and sustainability make it an attractive option for those seeking long-term results without the constraints of traditional dieting.

Week 2 Intermittent Fasting Exercises

The best way to start intermittent fasting (IF) is to approach it gradually and mindfully, allowing your body to adapt to the new eating pattern without feeling overwhelmed. Below are the steps and strategies that can help you start intermittent fasting effectively:

Choose the Right Fasting Schedule

There are several different intermittent fasting methods, so it's important to choose one that aligns with your lifestyle and goals. Some of the most popular include:

16:8 Method: Fast for 16 hours and eat within an 8-hour window. This is the most common and beginner-friendly approach.

12:12 Method: Fast for 12 hours and eat within a 12-hour window. This is a great starting point, especially if you're new to fasting.

5:2 Diet: Eat normally for five days of the week and significantly reduce calorie intake (around 500-600 calories) for two non-consecutive days.

24-Hour Fast: Fast for a full 24 hours once or twice a week (also called "Eat-Stop-Eat"). This method is more advanced and may not be ideal for beginners.

Alternate-Day Fasting: Fast every other day, which can be challenging for beginners but effective for more experienced fasters.

Best way to start: Begin with a more flexible schedule like the 12:12 or 16:8 method and slowly increase the fasting window as your body adjusts. This gradual approach helps prevent overwhelm and encourages long-term sustainability.

Ease into the Fasting Window

Rather than jumping straight into longer fasting periods, ease into it by gradually extending the time between your last meal of the day and your first meal the next day. For example:

Week 1: Fast for 12 hours (e.g., 8 p.m. to 8 a.m.).

Week 2: Extend the fasting window to 14 hours (e.g., 8 p.m. to 10 a.m.).

Week 3: Aim for 16 hours of fasting (e.g., 8 p.m. to 12 p.m.).

Best way to start: Gradually increase the fasting window to give your body time to adapt. This approach helps you avoid intense hunger pangs or energy dips that can occur when fasting for longer periods.

Stay Hydrated

Hydration is crucial during intermittent fasting. Drinking water, herbal teas, or black coffee (without added sugar or milk) can help stave off hunger, improve focus, and support overall well-being.

Best way to start: Drink plenty of water throughout the fasting period. Aim for at least 8 cups of water per day. Herbal teas and black coffee are also fasting-friendly, and they can help with appetite control.

Eat Balanced, Nutrient-Dense Meals

What you eat during your eating window is just as important as when you eat. Focus on nutrient-dense, whole foods that will keep you full and energized. Incorporate a balance of:

Healthy fats (e.g., avocado, nuts, olive oil)

Lean proteins (e.g., chicken, fish, legumes)

Complex carbohydrates (e.g., sweet potatoes, quinoa, brown rice)

Fiber-rich vegetables and fruits

Best way to start: Avoid processed foods and sugary snacks during your eating window. These can cause blood sugar spikes and lead to increased hunger. Instead, focus on nutrient-dense meals to keep you satisfied and nourished.

AWAKENED EATING

Listen to Your Body

It's important to tune into your body's signals as you start intermittent fasting. Some hunger is normal, but if you feel lightheaded, dizzy, or excessively fatigued, it's a sign that you may need to adjust your approach. It's okay to break your fast early or take a step back if necessary.

Best way to start: Start with shorter fasting periods and only extend your fasting window when you feel comfortable. If fasting feels too challenging or if you experience negative symptoms, listen to your body and make adjustments.

Start During a Calm Period

Starting intermittent fasting during a low-stress period can help you stay focused on making the transition smoothly. Beginning while on vacation or during a particularly busy or stressful time can make the process more difficult, as emotional or stress-related eating may arise.

Best way to start: Choose a time when your schedule allows for rest and consistency. For example, start on a weekend or a week when you don't have high-pressure commitments.

Manage Hunger with Distractions

During fasting, you may experience bouts of hunger, especially when you're first starting. Distracting yourself with non-food-related activities can help. Go for a walk, meditate, engage in a hobby, or dive into a work project.

Best way to start: Use hunger as a signal to engage in a productive activity. Often, hunger comes in waves, and distracting yourself will help you ride through the hunger pangs.

Avoid Overeating After Fasting

It can be tempting to overeat once you break your fast, but doing so can make you feel sluggish and negate some of the benefits of fasting. Instead, aim for controlled, portioned meals that are nutrient-dense and satisfying.

Best way to start: Break your fast with a small, balanced meal, such as a salad with lean protein or a smoothie with vegetables, protein, and healthy fats. This will help ease your digestive system back into eating mode without overwhelming it.

Be Flexible and Forgiving

Remember that intermittent fasting is not an all-or-nothing approach. It's okay to have days when you don't fast as planned, or when you need to adjust your eating window. The key to long-term success is consistency, not perfection.

Best way to start: Don't be hard on yourself if you slip up or feel the need to adjust your fasting window. Simply get back on track the next day. Flexibility is crucial for long-term adherence.

Get Support

Having a support system can make the transition into intermittent fasting much smoother. Whether it's joining an online community, following intermittent fasting influencers, or getting guidance from a health coach, support can provide motivation, encouragement, and accountability.

Best way to start: Share your intermittent fasting journey with a friend, join a fasting group, or seek out online communities where you can exchange tips, ask questions, and stay motivated.

Incorporate Emotional Practices

As intermittent fasting can sometimes trigger emotional eating patterns, especially when food has been used for comfort in the past, it's helpful to integrate emotional practices like mindfulness, meditation, or journaling into your routine.

Best way to start: Start your day with a positive mindset by meditating for a few minutes or writing down affirmations to stay mindful of your goals and emotional well-being during fasting.

Summary: The Best Way to Start Intermittent Fasting

Choose a beginner-friendly fasting schedule (e.g., 12:12 or 16:8 method).

Gradually extend your fasting window as you get more comfortable.

Stay hydrated and eat balanced, whole foods during your eating window.

Listen to your body and adjust your fasting schedule if needed.

Start during a calm period and use distractions to manage hunger.

Avoid overeating after fasting, and be flexible with yourself.

Get support from communities or friends and incorporate emotional practices like journaling or mindfulness to support your mental and emotional health.

By approaching intermittent fasting with a gradual, patient, and mindful strategy, you're more likely to succeed and experience the benefits without feeling overwhelmed.

Intermittent Fasting Meditation: Cultivating Patience and Self-Compassion

Find a quiet place where you won't be disturbed. Sit or lie down in a comfortable position. Close your eyes and begin by taking a few deep breaths. Let the breath flow naturally in and out, and start to settle into the present moment.

Feel your body supported by the surface beneath you. Take a moment to connect with your body, noticing how you feel right now. There's no need to change or judge these feelings—simply observe. Let your breath guide you, bringing awareness to any tension, hunger, or emotional sensations.

As you breathe in, silently say to yourself, "I am present."

As you breathe out, say, "I am grounded."

AWAKENED EATING

Let this grounding sensation spread through your body. Feel yourself anchored in the moment, calm and at ease, no matter what sensations or emotions arise.

Now, bring to mind your intention for intermittent fasting. What are you hoping to achieve? Whether it's for health, balance, or self-care, hold that intention gently in your heart.

Silently say to yourself, "I am choosing this journey with patience and care."

Feel the intention settling within you, creating a sense of commitment and purpose.

If you notice feelings of hunger, anxiety, or impatience, bring your awareness to those sensations. Imagine them as waves in the ocean, rising and falling naturally, without resistance. Know that just as the waves come and go, so too will the hunger and emotional discomfort pass.

As you breathe in, say, "I welcome this moment."

As you breathe out, say, "I release any tension."

If you feel any discomfort, place your hand on your heart and silently say, "It's okay. I am learning. I am growing." Feel the warmth of your hand as a symbol of self-compassion. Give yourself permission to feel whatever arises without judgment.

Now, visualize yourself on this intermittent fasting journey. Imagine moving through your day with ease and grace, feeling light and energized. Picture yourself calmly managing the fasting window, knowing you're making choices that nourish and strengthen your body.

As you continue breathing, visualize your body adapting, becoming more resilient and balanced with each breath. See yourself achieving your goals, feeling proud and empowered by your progress.

As you breathe in, say, "I am in control of my journey."

As you breathe out, say, "I trust my body and my choices."

Take a moment to express gratitude for your body and all it does for you. Even in moments of hunger or discomfort, your body is working to heal, strengthen, and renew itself.

Silently say, "Thank you, body, for supporting me."

Feel a sense of appreciation growing within you, extending from your heart throughout your body.

As you come to the end of this meditation, remind yourself of the importance of patience and flexibility on this journey. There may be days when it feels harder than others, and that's okay. Trust that you are making progress, and be kind to yourself when challenges arise.

Silently say, "I am patient with my progress."

Say, "I trust the process, and I am kind to myself."

Feel the sense of patience and trust fill your entire being. Know that you are doing something positive for yourself, and that every moment is part of your growth.

AWAKENED EATING

Take a few more deep breaths, allowing peace and calm to fill your mind and body. Let go of any tension or doubts, and feel a sense of clarity about your path forward.

As you breathe in, say, "I am at peace."

As you breathe out, say, "I am whole."

When you feel ready, slowly bring your awareness back to the present moment. Gently wiggle your fingers and toes, and when you're ready, open your eyes. Carry the sense of patience, self-compassion, and peace with you as you continue your intermittent fasting journey

SLOWING DOWN MY EATING

I've always been a fast eater. Growing up in a busy household, meals were often rushed, and it became second nature for me to scarf down food without thinking much about it. It wasn't until I started experiencing frequent bloating and indigestion that I realized something needed to change. That's when I stumbled upon the concept of mindful eating, specifically the idea of slowing down and savoring each bite.

One night, after a particularly long day, I decided to give it a try. Instead of mindlessly scrolling through my phone or watching TV while eating dinner, I set the table nicely—something I rarely did just for myself. I turned off all distractions and sat down, determined to be fully present for the meal.

At first, it felt strange. My instinct was to eat quickly, as usual, but I reminded myself to slow down. I decided to follow the advice I'd read: chew each bite 20-30 times. On my first bite, I realized how little attention I usually paid to my food. The textures, the flavors—it was like I was truly tasting my dinner for the first time.

I focused on each chew, noticing how the food transformed in my mouth, the way the flavors deepened with each bite. To my surprise, the simple act of chewing more thoroughly made the food taste better. I had always heard that digestion starts in the mouth, but this was the first time I truly understood what that meant.

Next, I tried taking smaller bites. I cut my food into smaller pieces, something I hadn't thought much about before. It slowed me down naturally, making it easier to chew thoroughly and enjoy the process. I even switched to using smaller utensils, which felt a bit silly at first, but it worked. The smaller spoon made me more conscious of each bite, and I found myself getting fuller faster, without needing to finish the entire plate.

One of the hardest adjustments was putting my fork down between bites. It felt like an awkward pause, but as I sat there, I realized how much time I usually spent shoveling the next bite in before even finishing the one in my mouth. For the first time, I was allowing myself to fully experience the food without rushing through it.

As I continued eating this way, I started noticing how relaxed I felt. The entire meal became a calming ritual rather than a rushed necessity. It was as if by slowing down, I was giving my body the time it needed to process not just the food but also the moment. My stomach felt lighter, and I no longer experienced the uncomfortable fullness that used to come from eating too quickly.

Over the next few weeks, I made these mindful eating habits part of my daily routine. I took time to create a peaceful eating environment, even if it was just setting the table and lighting a candle for myself. I continued to chew slowly, take smaller bites, and put my utensils

WEEK 3 SLOWING DOWN

Slowing down and savoring each bite of your food can enhance your eating experience, improve digestion, and help you become more mindful of what and how much you're eating.

Here are some practical strategies to help you eat more slowly and mindfully:

Create a Calm Eating Environment

- Turn off the TV, put away your phone, and create a peaceful environment.
- Set the Table: Arrange your eating space nicely to make the meal feel special.

Count Chews

- Aim to chew each bite at least 20-30 times. This helps break down the food better and slows down your eating pace.
- Textures and Flavors: Pay attention to the different textures and flavors in your mouth.

Take Smaller Bites

- Cut Food into Smaller Pieces
- Smaller bites make it easier to chew thoroughly.
- Use Smaller Utensils: Smaller forks or spoons can help you take smaller bites.

Put Down Utensils

- After each bite, put your fork or spoon down and take a moment to enjoy the flavors.
- Drink water between bites. Drinking water between bites can help you slow down and also aids digestion.

Engage Your Senses

- Look at Your Food: Notice the colors, shapes, and presentation.
- Smell Your Food: Take a moment to appreciate the aroma before taking a bite.
- Listen to Your Food: Pay attention to the sounds your food makes as you chew.

Practice Mindful Breathing

- Deep Breaths: Before starting your meal, take a few deep breaths to relax.
- Breathe Between Bites: Take a deep breath after swallowing and before taking the next bite.

Eat with Others Engage in Conversation

- Engage in conversation with your dining companions, which naturally slows down your eating pace.
- Pacing: Try to match the eating pace of the slowest eater at the table.

Set a Timer Timed Meals

Set a timer for 20-30 minutes and aim to stretch your meal to last that entire duration.

Reflect on Your Meal, have a Mid-Meal Check-In

Halfway through your meal, pause and check in with your hunger and fullness levels.

Post-Meal Reflection

After finishing, take a moment to reflect on how you feel physically and emotionally.

Mindful Eating Exercise: Raisin Meditation

This exercise is a classic way to practice eating mindfully and slowing down.

Choose a Raisin

Take a single raisin and hold it in your hand.

Look at it closely, noticing its shape, color, and texture.

Smell the Raisin

Bring it to your nose and take in its aroma.

Feel its texture between your fingers.

Place in Mouth

Put the raisin in your mouth without chewing. Notice how it feels.

Chew Slowly

Chew the raisin very slowly, paying attention to the taste and texture. Notice how the flavors change as you chew.

Swallow Mindfully

After chewing thoroughly, swallow the raisin and notice the sensations in your throat and body.

Slowing down and savoring each bite is a practice that takes time to develop. By incorporating these strategies and exercises into your daily routine, you can cultivate a more mindful approach to eating, leading to greater enjoyment and better health.

WEEK 3 EXERCISES

Breathing Meditation Purpose:

To center yourself and become present before eating.

Sit in a chair or on the floor with a straight back.

Gently close your eyes and take a few deep breaths.

Notice the sensation of your breath entering and leaving your nostrils.

Count each inhale and exhale up to ten, then start over.

Continue for 5-10 Minutes: If your mind wanders, gently bring it back to the breath.

Choose a Small Piece of Food: It could be a raisin, a piece of chocolate, or a slice of fruit.

Examine the Food: Look at it closely, noting its color, texture, and shape.

Smell the Food: Bring it to your nose and take in its aroma.

Touch the Food: Feel the texture with your fingers.

Take a Small Bite: Notice the flavor, texture, and temperature.

Chew Slowly: Chew thoroughly and notice the sensations in your mouth.

Swallow: Pay attention to the act of swallowing and how your body feels.

Reflect: Take a moment to reflect on the experience.

Continue to journal just like Week 1. At some point during the week take time to journal about the on Daily Eating Routine:

- Describe your typical eating routine.

Awakened Eating

- How often do you eat mindfully?
- Hunger and Fullness: How do you know when you're hungry?
- How do you know when you're full?
- Emotional Triggers:
- Are there any emotions that trigger you to eat?
- How do you handle them?
- Food Choices:
- What guides your food choices?
- Is it convenience, nutrition, or something else?
-
- Do you eat while watching TV, working, or using your phone?
- How does it affect your eating experience?
- How often do you think about its journey from farm to table?
- Gratitude: How can you cultivate a sense of gratitude for your food?
- Mindful Cooking: Describe how you can bring mindfulness into the process of preparing meals.
- Cultural Significance: What foods are significant in your culture or family?
- How do they connect you to your heritage?
- How does eating with others affect your mindfulness and enjoyment of food?

Meditation on Slowing Down When You Eat

Introduction Find a quiet and comfortable place to sit. Whether you're about to begin your meal or you've just sat down with a snack, allow yourself to relax. Close your eyes gently and take a deep breath in through your nose, filling your lungs. Hold for a moment, and then exhale slowly through your mouth, releasing any tension you may be holding in your body. Let your mind settle into this present moment, free of distractions.

Setting an Intention As you breathe, set an intention for this meal or snack: to eat slowly, mindfully, and with gratitude. Allow yourself to acknowledge that you are here, in this moment, to nourish both your body and your mind. Remind yourself that there is no rush. Today, you will savor each bite, each flavor, each sensation.

Connecting with Your Food Now, take a moment to look at the food in front of you. Whether it's a small snack or a full meal, notice the colors, shapes, and textures. How does it appear to you? Allow your eyes to fully engage with the food before you. Take a deep breath in, and as you do, inhale the aroma. What do you notice? How does it smell? Engage all of your senses as you prepare to slow down and truly experience your food.

The First Bite When you're ready, take your first bite. Let it be small. As you place the food in your mouth, pay attention to how it feels against your tongue. Notice the texture before you begin to chew. As you chew, count slowly, aiming for 20-30 chews. With each chew, notice how the flavors unfold. Is there a subtle sweetness? A bit of salt? Maybe an unexpected texture? Let each bite become a moment of curiosity and discovery.

Pausing Between Bites Once you've finished chewing and have swallowed, pause. Set your utensils down, or rest your hands on your lap. Take a deep breath, feeling the air expand your belly. Exhale slowly, letting your body relax between bites. Notice how your body feels in this pause. Does your mind want to rush forward? Acknowledge that feeling and gently guide your focus

AWAKENED EATING

back to this moment, this bite, this breath. There is no need to hurry.

Engaging with the Meal As you continue, repeat this process with each bite. Take your time. Chew thoroughly, savoring each flavor and texture. Between bites, breathe deeply and mindfully. Allow each breath to ground you in the present. If your mind begins to wander or rush ahead, gently bring it back to the act of eating slowly. You are in no hurry. You have all the time you need.

Reflecting on Hunger and Fullness As you eat, notice how your body feels. Are you starting to feel satisfied? Are you still hungry? Check in with your hunger and fullness levels, knowing that you are in tune with your body's needs. Let these cues guide you in deciding how much more to eat, or when to stop.

Post-Meal Reflection As your meal comes to an end, take a moment to sit in stillness. Close your eyes once again and take a deep breath. How does your body feel after eating slowly and mindfully? How does your mind feel? Notice any emotions or sensations that arise. Reflect on how slowing down allowed you to experience the meal more fully, with gratitude and awareness.

Closing Before you go about the rest of your day, take one final deep breath. Let a sense of calm and peace fill your body. Carry this practice of slowing down with you, knowing that whenever you choose to, you can return to this mindful state—whether eating, walking, or simply breathing. You are in control of the pace of your life, and by slowing down, you can find a deeper connection with yourself and the present moment.

APPRECIATING MY FOOD

Growing up, I never really thought about where my food came from. I was raised in a fast-paced household where meals were often rushed, and the focus was more on getting fed quickly than truly appreciating the process. It wasn't until I moved out on my own and began preparing my own meals that I started to think about the journey my food took to get to my plate. This shift in awareness completely changed how I approached food, cooking, and eating.

One afternoon, as I stood in my kitchen chopping vegetables for a simple stir-fry, I found myself reflecting on the origins of each ingredient. The vibrant green peppers, the crisp carrots, and the fragrant garlic all had their own stories. I imagined the farmers who grew them, the hands that harvested them, and the journey they took to reach my local grocery store. For the first time, I acknowledged how much effort and care went into bringing that food to my table.

This newfound awareness made me feel a deep sense of gratitude, not just for the meal I was about to prepare, but for the entire process. I began taking a moment before each meal to express silent gratitude—sometimes in the form of a thought, and other times, a brief prayer. It felt grounding, like I was connecting to something bigger than myself. To reinforce this practice, I started keeping a gratitude journal, jotting down small notes about the meals I had enjoyed, whether it was the freshness of a particular ingredient or the joy of sharing food with a friend.

With each meal, I began to appreciate the visual aspects of my food more as well. I noticed the colors of the ingredients, the way they changed as I cooked them, and the aromas that filled my kitchen. Before I would even take a bite, I would pause to inhale the scent of the meal, marveling at how the different flavors and textures would come together. These simple acts turned meals into experiences, where every bite felt like a reward.

I also became more curious about the origins of my food. I started learning about the nutritional benefits of different ingredients and began to appreciate foods I had once taken for granted, like the rich flavor of quinoa or the depth of spices in a curry. I even explored the cultural significance of various dishes, learning how certain foods were traditionally prepared and why they were cherished in different parts of the world.

Cooking, which had once felt like a chore, became a mindful practice. I began approaching each meal with intention, focusing on each step without distractions. The rhythm of chopping vegetables, stirring a sauce, or kneading dough became meditative. There was a simple pleasure in preparing food that I hadn't noticed before, and I found myself looking forward to the process as much as the meal itself.

When it came time to eat, I adopted the habit of slowing down. Rather than rushing through meals, I made a point to chew slowly and savor each bite. I stopped multitasking, no more eating in

BETHANY ORRICK

front of the TV or scrolling through my phone. Instead, I focused on the meal in front of me, fully immersed in the flavors and textures. Each bite became an opportunity to connect with the food, and I found myself feeling more satisfied, both physically and emotionally.

Sharing meals with others also took on new meaning. Whenever I had friends or family over for dinner, we would talk about the food—not just how it tasted, but the effort and love that went into preparing it. These conversations brought us closer, making each meal a shared experience of gratitude and connection.

Over time, I also became more attuned to my body's needs. I learned to eat when I was hungry and stop when I was full, trusting that my body would tell me what it needed. I focused on nourishing myself with foods that made me feel good, both physically and mentally. This shift in mindset helped me develop a healthier relationship with food—one where I no longer ate out of habit or stress, but out of respect for my body and appreciation for the food itself.

Looking back, I realize how transformative these practices have been. By slowing down, savoring my food, and cultivating gratitude, I've turned something as simple as eating into a mindful, fulfilling experience. It's no longer just about fueling my body—it's about connecting to the earth, the people who provide my food, and the joy of sharing it with others.

WEEK 4 APPRECIATING YOUR FOOD:

Involves recognizing the effort and processes that bring food to your table, savoring its flavors and textures, and cultivating a sense of gratitude for the nourishment it provides. Here are some practical ways to appreciate your food more deeply.

Acknowledge the Journey of Your Food

- Consider where your food comes from, including the farmers, animals, and natural resources involved.
- Appreciate the work of those who planted, harvested, transported, and prepared your food.

Practice Gratitude

- Take a moment before each meal to express gratitude. This can be a silent thought, a prayer, or a spoken acknowledgment.
- Keep a Gratitude Journal: Write down what you're grateful for related to your meals, such as specific ingredients, the people who shared the meal with you, or the experience of cooking.

Visual Appreciation:

- Notice the colors, shapes, and presentation of your food.
- Take a moment to inhale the aromas before you begin eating.

- Feel the textures of your food with your hands and in your mouth.
- Savor the flavors fully, identifying different tastes and how they blend together.

Learn About Your Food

- Learn about the nutritional benefits and origins of the ingredients in your meals.
- Understand the cultural significance and traditional preparations of different foods.

Cook Mindfully

- Focus on the process of cooking without distractions, paying attention to each step.
- Take pleasure in the act of preparing food, from chopping vegetables to stirring a pot.

Eat MindfullySlow Down

- Take your time to chew and savor each bite.
- Avoid multitasking while eating. Instead, concentrate on the meal and the sensations it brings.

Share Meals Connect with Others

- Share meals with family and friends to enhance the experience and appreciation.
- Talk about the flavors, textures, and the effort put into preparing the meal.

Respect Your Body's Needs

- Eat when you're hungry and stop when you're full, honoring your body's signals.
- Select foods that provide the nutrients your body needs to thrive.

WEEK 4 EXERCISES

Continue to journal as you have been, but now add the following:

Food Appreciation Journal

- Each day, write down one food item you ate and reflect on its journey and nutritional benefits.
- Describe the sensory experience of eating that food—its taste, texture, and aroma.
- Write a few sentences about why you're grateful for that food.

Gratitude Meditation

Find a quiet space and sit comfortably.

Close Your Eyes

Take a few deep breaths to center yourself.

Imagine the journey of your food from the farm to your plate. Picture the farmers, the transport, the market, and the cooking process.

Silently express gratitude for each part of this journey.Open Your Open your eyes and start your meal with a sense of appreciation.

MINDFUL EATING PRACTICE

- Create a calm and pleasant eating environment.
- Start with a small portion of food, such as a piece of fruit or a small snack.
- Use all your senses to explore the food before taking a bite.
- Chew each bite thoroughly and notice the flavors and textures.
- After finishing, take a moment to reflect on the experience and the food's journey.

Appreciating your food is about more than just enjoying its taste. It's about recognizing the effort and resources that bring food to your table, engaging your senses fully, and cultivating gratitude for the nourishment and pleasure it provides. By incorporating these practices into your daily routine, you can develop a deeper connection with your food and enhance your overall well-being.

ENGAGING ALL MY SENSES

I'll never forget the first time I truly engaged all of my senses in the act of eating. It was a regular weeknight, and I had decided to prepare one of my favorite meals—roasted vegetables with a side of quinoa and a lemony tahini dressing. Normally, I would rush through the preparation and eat quickly while watching TV or scrolling through my phone. But that night, I wanted to try something different: I decided to experience my meal with all my senses, fully immersing myself in the process of eating.

It began with sight. As I laid the vegetables—bright orange carrots, deep purple beets, and green broccoli—on the baking sheet, I took a moment to appreciate the vibrant colors. I thought about how each color represented different nutrients that would nourish my body. Once the vegetables were roasted and plated, I noticed how the rich, caramelized edges contrasted beautifully with the fresh, crisp green of the parsley I sprinkled on top. It was as though I was looking at a work of art, and just seeing the plate made me excited to eat.

Next came the smell. As I brought the plate closer to my face, I closed my eyes and inhaled deeply. The sweet, earthy aroma of the roasted vegetables mixed with the tang of the lemon tahini

AWAKENED EATING

dressing. I could pick out the faint smokiness from the roasting and the citrusy brightness of the lemon. With each breath, I felt more connected to the meal, almost as if I was mentally preparing my taste buds for the flavors to come.

When I finally took my first bite, I paid attention to the texture of the food in my hands. I used my fingers to pick up a piece of roasted carrot, feeling its smooth, slightly charred surface. It was soft yet firm. I bit into it slowly, focusing on how it felt in my mouth. The inside was tender, contrasting with the slight crispness of the outer layer. Each bite felt deliberate, and I noticed a creamy element from the tahini dressing that coated my tongue, adding an extra layer of satisfaction to the experience.

Even the sound of the food added to my enjoyment. The vegetables didn't make much noise on their own, but the crackle of the roasting pan earlier had built my anticipation for the meal. When I ate the quinoa, I could hear a faint crunch with every bite. It was subtle, but there was something comforting about the sound, as if it was a reminder of the freshness and simplicity of the ingredients.

And then there was the taste. I took my time with each bite, letting the food linger in my mouth. I noticed the sweetness of the carrots, the slight bitterness of the beets, and the umami richness from the roasted broccoli. The lemon tahini dressing added a creamy, tangy contrast that brought the whole dish together. Each flavor stood out on its own but also complemented the others in a way that was deeply satisfying. It felt like I was tasting this dish for the first time, even though I had made it dozens of times before.

By the end of the meal, I realized how much more enjoyable eating could be when I involved all my senses. I felt fully satisfied— not just because the food was nourishing, but because I had experienced it on a deeper level. I wasn't just eating to fuel my body; I was engaging in a sensory experience that allowed me to appreciate the textures, flavors, and aromas in a way I hadn't before.

From that day forward, I made a conscious effort to engage my senses more during meals. Whether it's the sound of sizzling onions in a pan or the bright, fresh scent of herbs, I've come to see that food is so much more than just fuel. It's a full-body experience, one that can bring joy, comfort, and a sense of connection to both the ingredients and the act of eating itself.

AWAKENED EATING

WEEK 5 ENGAGING ALL YOUR SENSES

Engaging in all your senses to fully experience your food

Enhances the pleasure of eating and helps you become more mindful. Here's how you can involve each of your senses in the eating experience:

Sight

- Notice the vibrant or subtle colors of your food. Different colors can indicate different nutrients and flavors.
- Take a moment to appreciate how the food is arranged on your plate. A beautifully presented meal can enhance your anticipation and enjoyment.

Smell

- Before taking a bite, bring the food close to your nose and take a deep breath. Notice the different aromas and how they make you feel.
- Try to pick out individual scents. For example, in a dish with garlic, tomatoes, and basil, see if you can identify each aroma.

Touch

- Use your hands to feel the texture of the food. Is it smooth, rough, soft, or firm?

- Pay attention to how the food feels in your mouth. Is it creamy, crunchy, or chewy?

Hearing

- Notice the sounds your food makes as you eat. Does it crunch, crackle, or sizzle?
- When preparing food, listen to the sounds of chopping, sizzling, or bubbling. These can enhance your anticipation and connection to the meal.

Taste

- Take small bites and let the food linger in your mouth. Notice the primary tastes (sweet, salty, sour, bitter, umami) and how they interact.
- Try to identify different flavors in a dish. How do they complement or contrast with each other?

WEEK 5 EXERCISE:

The Mindful Bite

- Choose a Small Piece of Food: Select a small piece of food that you enjoy, such as a piece of fruit, chocolate, or a vegetable.
- Engage Your Senses:
- Look at the food and notice its color, shape, and any details.
- Bring it to your nose and take in its aroma.
- Feel the texture of the food in your fingers.

AWAKENED EATING

- If appropriate, notice any sounds the food makes when you handle it.
- Slowly take a small bite, but do not chew immediately. Notice the initial taste and texture.
- Begin to chew slowly, paying attention to how the flavors and textures change. Notice any sounds the food makes in your mouth.
- As you swallow, be aware of the sensation of the food moving down your throat.
- Take a moment to reflect on the experience. How did engaging all your senses change your perception of the food?

By engaging all your senses, you can transform the act of eating into a rich and enjoyable experience. This mindfulness practice not only enhances your appreciation for food but also helps you eat more slowly and intentionally. With practice, engaging your senses can become a natural part of your eating routine, leading to greater satisfaction and a deeper connection with your food.

Becoming non-judgmental towards our foods and eating habits involves cultivating a mindset of acceptance and compassion. Here are some strategies to help you adopt a non-judgmental attitude:

Meditation on Engaging All Your Senses While Eating

Introduction Begin by sitting in a comfortable, quiet space with your meal in front of you. Take a moment to close your eyes and take a deep breath in through your nose, filling your lungs fully. Hold for a moment, then exhale slowly, releasing any tension or stress. Allow yourself to fully arrive in this moment, free from distractions and focused on the present. Set the intention to experience your meal mindfully by engaging all of your senses.

Sight Gently open your eyes and bring your awareness to the sight of your food. Notice the colors on your plate. Are they bright and vibrant, or more subtle and calming? Take a moment to appreciate how the food is arranged. How does the presentation make you feel? Does it spark joy or anticipation? Let your eyes rest on the details—textures, shapes, and patterns. Allow yourself to savor the experience visually before taking your first bite.

Smell Before picking up your utensils, bring the food close to your nose. Take a deep, mindful breath, inhaling the aromas. What do you notice? Are there strong, distinct smells, or more subtle and delicate fragrances? Take your time to explore the complexity of the scent. Can you identify individual aromas, such as garlic, citrus, or herbs? Let the scent deepen your connection to the food and awaken your anticipation for the first bite.

Touch Now, use your hands to feel the texture of the food, if appropriate. Is it smooth, soft, or firm? Let your fingers explore the surface, noticing the sensations. When you place the food in your mouth, shift your focus to how it feels against your tongue. Is it creamy, crunchy, chewy, or light? Pay close attention to the way the texture changes as you chew. Savor each sensation, letting it enhance your eating experience.

The First Bite With all your senses engaged, take your first bite slowly. Feel the texture, notice the flavors as they emerge, and allow yourself to fully experience this moment. As you chew, be mindful of how your senses continue to interact with the food—the taste intensifying, the texture transforming, the scent lingering in the background.

AWAKENED EATING

Engaging All Senses as You Continue As you move through your meal, continue to involve all of your senses. Notice the colors on your plate with each bite, take small moments to appreciate the aroma, feel the texture with your hands or in your mouth, and savor how each sense contributes to the full experience of eating. Let the meal become a meditation in itself, an opportunity to be fully present with your food.

Reflection When your meal is finished, take a deep breath and close your eyes once again. Reflect on the experience of engaging all your senses. How did it change your connection with the food? How did it enhance your enjoyment? How do you feel now, both physically and emotionally?

Take one last deep breath, and as you exhale, carry this sense of mindfulness and sensory awareness with you throughout the rest of your day. Eating with all your senses allows you to not only nourish your body but also to find greater joy and presence in each moment.

Closing As you return to your day, remember that you can always come back to this practice. By slowing down and engaging your senses, you can bring mindfulness and gratitude to each meal, making eating a richer and more fulfilling experience.

BECOMING NON-JUDGMENTAL

For a long time, my relationship with food was defined by strict rules and a cycle of guilt. I had fallen into the habit of labeling foods as "good" or "bad," and if I ate something from the "bad" list, I would beat myself up over it for days. It felt like every meal was a test of willpower, and I often failed, leaving me feeling defeated and ashamed. But the turning point came when I realized I needed to cultivate more awareness, practice self-compassion, and adopt a non-restrictive mindset around food.

One moment stands out clearly in my memory. It was a Friday night, and I had been trying to eat "perfectly" all week. I decided to treat myself to some pizza with friends. But halfway through the meal, the old, judgmental thoughts started creeping in: "You shouldn't be eating this. You'll regret it tomorrow." I started to feel guilty, thinking that I had undone all the "good" I had done throughout the week.

But instead of spiraling into shame, I took a step back and practiced something I had recently learned—awareness. I acknowledged the critical thoughts without letting them take control. I noticed them for what they were: just thoughts, not facts. Instead of punishing

AWAKENED EATING

myself for having those thoughts, I simply observed them and let them pass, without letting them dictate how I felt about myself.

In that moment, I also practiced self-compassion. I reminded myself that I wasn't "bad" for enjoying pizza. Everyone indulges from time to time, and it doesn't define their worth or health. I imagined how I would respond if a close friend came to me feeling guilty about eating pizza. I would never shame her—I would tell her it's okay to enjoy the food she loves, and one meal doesn't undo all the positive habits she's built. So why couldn't I offer that same kindness to myself? I did. I forgave myself for the guilt I was feeling and chose to focus on the enjoyment of the evening rather than the food I had eaten.

This was a pivotal moment in shifting my mindset. I realized that labeling foods as "good" or "bad" was what perpetuated the cycle of guilt. So, I decided to remove those labels from my vocabulary altogether. Instead of seeing pizza as a "bad" food that I should avoid, I reframed it as something I could enjoy in moderation. Over time, I learned to adopt a more balanced approach, where no food was off-limits but where I also prioritized nourishing my body with a variety of whole, nutritious foods. I found that when I allowed myself to enjoy all kinds of food without guilt, I was much less likely to overeat or feel out of control around those foods.

Another key change was shifting the language I used around food. In the past, if I indulged in dessert or comfort food, I would say things like, "I was bad today" or "I ruined my diet." But I began replacing those phrases with more neutral or positive language. Instead of saying, "I was bad for eating that," I would say, "I enjoyed that meal" or "I chose to indulge, and that's okay."

BETHANY ORRICK

This simple shift in language made a big difference in how I felt about myself and my food choices.

As I continued to practice self-compassion and cultivate awareness, I noticed a huge improvement in my overall well-being. I no longer felt chained to the guilt and shame that used to accompany my food choices. Instead, I felt free to enjoy food, trusting that I could make balanced decisions without punishing myself. If I overate or chose a food that didn't make me feel great afterward, I learned to forgive myself and move on, knowing that one moment didn't define my health or my worth.

This journey of cultivating awareness and practicing self-compassion has completely transformed my relationship with food. I now approach eating with a sense of ease and enjoyment, free from the rigid rules and guilt that used to dominate my thoughts. It's been a liberating shift, and it has allowed me to nourish not just my body, but my mind and spirit as well.

AWAKENED EATING

WEEK 6 STRATEGIES TO BECOME NON-JUDGMENTAL

Cultivate Awareness

- Pay attention to the thoughts that arise when you eat or think about food. Recognize any judgmental or critical thoughts.
- When you notice a judgmental thought, acknowledge it without reacting to it. Simply observe it and let it pass.

Practice Self-Compassion

- Treat yourself with the same kindness and understanding you would offer a friend. Remember that everyone has moments of indulgence or less-than-perfect eating habits.
- If you overeat or make a food choice you later regret, forgive yourself and move on. Dwelling on it only perpetuates negative feelings.

Adopt a Non-Restrictive Mindset

- Instead of labeling foods as "good" or "bad," consider all foods as permissible in moderation. This reduces the sense of guilt associated with eating certain foods.
- Aim for a balanced diet that includes a variety of foods. Allow yourself to enjoy treats without feeling guilty.

Shift Your Language

- Use positive and neutral language when talking about food and eating. Replace phrases like "I was bad for eating that" with "I enjoyed eating that."
- Avoid labeling foods as "junk" or "bad." Instead, consider them as occasional treats or indulgences.

WEEK 6 EXERCISES

Mindful Eating Practices

- Focus on the act of eating, paying attention to the flavors, textures, and sensations. This can help you appreciate your food without judgment.
- Eating slowly allows you to savor your food and listen to your body's signals, fostering a more mindful and non-judgmental approach.

Reflect on Your Relationship with Food Journal

- Keep a journal to explore your thoughts and feelings about food and eating. This can help you identify patterns and work through any negative emotions.
- Consider how cultural, social, and familial influences have shaped your attitudes toward food. Understanding these influences can help you reframe your thoughts.

AWAKENED EATING

Seek Support

- If you find it challenging to adopt a non-judgmental attitude, consider talking to a therapist or dietitian who specializes in mindful eating or intuitive eating.
- Engage with communities or support groups that promote non-judgmental and mindful eating practices.

Non-Judgmental Reflection

- After a meal, write down any judgmental thoughts you had about the food or your eating habits.
- For each judgmental thought, write a compassionate and understanding response. For example, if you wrote, "I shouldn't have eaten that dessert," respond with, "It's okay to enjoy a dessert sometimes. It's part of a balanced approach to eating."
- Reflect on how it feels to replace judgment with acceptance. Notice any changes in your mood or attitude towards food.

Mindful Eating Journal

- Keep a daily journal of your eating experiences, focusing on the sensory aspects of eating without judgment.
- Write about the taste, texture, and enjoyment of the food without labeling it as "good" or "bad."
- Record any emotions you feel before, during, and after eating. Aim to observe these emotions without judgment.

Adopting a non-judgmental attitude towards food and eating habits takes practice and patience. By cultivating awareness, practicing self-compassion, and embracing mindful eating, you can develop a healthier and more positive relationship with food.

BETHANY ORRICK

Remember, it's about progress, not perfection, and every step towards a more accepting and compassionate mindset is a step in the right direction.

Meditation on Cultivating Awareness and Self-Compassion in Eating

Introduction Find a quiet, comfortable space where you can sit undisturbed. Close your eyes gently and bring your attention to your breath. Take a slow, deep breath in through your nose, feeling the air fill your lungs, and then exhale softly through your mouth, releasing any tension. With each breath, allow yourself to settle more fully into the present moment. Set the intention for this meditation to cultivate awareness, self-compassion, and a non-restrictive mindset around food and eating.

Awareness of Thoughts Begin by bringing your awareness to your thoughts, especially those related to food or eating. What do you notice? Do any judgmental or critical thoughts arise? Perhaps thoughts about what you should or shouldn't eat, or feelings of guilt about past food choices? Simply observe these thoughts without judgment. Notice them as they come and go, like clouds passing across the sky. Remind yourself that thoughts are just thoughts; they do not define you, and you are not obligated to act on them.

Acknowledging Judgment Without Reacting When you notice a judgmental or self-critical thought, pause. Instead of reacting or letting the thought spiral, gently acknowledge its presence. Say to yourself, "I see this thought," and then allow it to pass. With each breath, let the thought drift away, releasing its hold on you. Return your focus to the present, to the calm and peaceful space you are creating within yourself. You are not defined by these passing thoughts.

Practicing Self-Compassion Now, bring your attention to the idea of self-compassion. Imagine speaking to yourself with the same kindness and understanding you would offer a close friend. If you've ever had a moment of overeating or made a food choice you later regretted, remind yourself that everyone has these moments. Place your hand gently over your heart, and with each breath, offer yourself forgiveness and grace. Whisper softly to yourself, "I forgive myself. I release this moment with love and compassion."

Adopting a Non-Restrictive Mindset As you continue breathing deeply, reflect on the concept of food as a source of nourishment and enjoyment. Instead of labeling foods as "good" or "bad," bring your attention to the idea of balance. All foods are permissible in moderation. Visualize yourself enjoying a balanced variety of foods, including occasional treats, without guilt or shame. Feel the sense of freedom that comes from releasing the restrictive mindset. You are choosing to nourish your body and mind with kindness and balance.

Shifting Your Language Take a moment to reflect on the language you use when talking about food. Notice any patterns of negative or judgmental words. As you observe these thoughts, imagine replacing those words with neutral or positive phrases. Instead of "I was bad for eating that," try saying, "I enjoyed eating that." Instead of labeling foods as "junk" or "bad," consider them as occasional treats. With each breath, feel the weight of negative language lift, replaced by a sense of peace and acceptance.

Reflection As this meditation draws to a close, reflect on how it feels to cultivate awareness, self-compassion, and a non-restrictive mindset around food. How does your body feel? How does your mind feel? Allow a sense of ease and peace to settle over you, knowing that you are free to make food choices from a place of balance and self-kindness. Let go of any lingering judgment and embrace a more compassionate relationship with food and yourself.

Closing Take one final, deep breath in, filling yourself with self-compassion, and exhale slowly, releasing any residual negativity. When you are ready, gently open your eyes. Carry this sense of awareness and compassion with you throughout your day, knowing that each meal, each snack, is an opportunity to practice kindness toward yourself. You are worthy of love and balance, both in how you eat and in how you speak to yourself.

My Gratitude Journey

One evening, after a long day, I sat down at the dinner table, feeling worn out and disconnected from the day's events. In front of me was a simple meal—grilled chicken, roasted vegetables, and quinoa. Normally, I would have eaten it quickly, barely noticing the details of the meal, eager to move on to something else. But that night, something made me pause. I remembered reading about a practice of mindfulness and gratitude around food, and I decided to give it a try.

I found a quiet space in my dining room, away from distractions. I turned off the TV, put my phone on silent, and sat comfortably at the table. Closing my eyes, I took a few deep breaths, letting go of the day's stress with each exhale. As my breathing slowed, I felt a sense of calm washing over me, as if I was grounding myself in the present moment for the first time that day.

AWAKENED EATING

With my eyes still closed, I began to visualize the journey of the food before me. I imagined the farmers tending to their fields, growing the vegetables that now sat on my plate. I saw rows of colorful produce, swaying gently in the breeze, and the hard-working hands that harvested each piece. I pictured the chickens raised on a farm, their care and the people responsible for ensuring their well-being. I thought about the markets and grocery stores that stocked the ingredients, the people who transported the food across miles, and the workers who organized it on shelves.

As I moved through this mental journey, I felt a growing appreciation for each person and process involved. It wasn't something I usually thought about, but visualizing the journey made me realize just how many steps were required to bring that simple meal to my plate. I silently expressed gratitude for each part of this journey—the farmers, the transportation workers, the markets, and even myself for preparing the meal. It gave me a sense of connection to the food and the world around me that I hadn't felt before.

Finally, before opening my eyes, I set an intention. I promised myself that I would bring more mindfulness and gratitude to my meals moving forward. I wanted to make eating less of a rushed task and more of an experience—one where I could appreciate not just the flavors, but the entire process that brought the food to me.

When I opened my eyes and began to eat, everything felt different. The food tasted richer, more vibrant. The textures were more pronounced, and I found myself savoring each bite. The meal became an experience, not just a necessity.

From that night on, I made a point to find moments of stillness before meals, even if just for a minute or two. I would breathe, visualize, express gratitude, and set an intention. This simple practice shifted the way I interacted with food. It made each meal more meaningful, and it deepened my sense of connection to the world that sustains me. I no longer took for granted the journey from earth to plate, and in doing so, I cultivated a greater appreciation for the nourishment food provides—both physically and spiritually.

WEEK 7 EXERCISES GRATITUDE AND CONNECTION

Find a Quiet Space

Sit comfortably and close your eyes

Deep Breaths

Take a few deep breaths to center yourself

Visualize Your Food's Journey

Picture the journey of your food from the earth to the plate. Visualize the farmers, the transportation, the markets, and the preparation.

Express Gratitude

Silently express gratitude for each part of this journey.

Set an Intention

Set an intention to bring more mindfulness and gratitude to your future meals.

CLOSING MEDITATION: EMBRACING INNER STRENGTH FOR HEALTHY CHOICES

Welcome to this closing meditation. We'll take this time to reflect on the journey toward making healthy food choices, tapping into our inner strength, and cultivating mindfulness and self-compassion. Find a comfortable position, either sitting or lying down, in a quiet space where you won't be disturbed.

Take a moment to settle into your chosen position. Close your eyes and take a few deep breaths. Inhale deeply through your nose, filling your lungs completely, and then exhale slowly through your mouth. With each breath, allow yourself to relax more deeply, releasing any tension or stress from your body and mind.

Begin by grounding yourself in the present moment. Feel the connection between your body and the surface supporting you. Notice the sensation of your feet touching the ground or the support beneath you. Allow this sense of grounding to bring you fully into the here and now.

AWAKENED EATING

Gently bring your awareness to your body. Starting from the top of your head, slowly scan down through your body, noticing any areas of tension or discomfort. As you breathe in, imagine sending your breath to those areas, inviting relaxation and ease. As you exhale, release any remaining tension, allowing your body to feel more relaxed and at peace.

Now, bring your attention to your breath. Notice the natural rhythm of your breathing without trying to change it. Simply observe the rise and fall of your chest and abdomen with each inhale and exhale. Allow your breath to become a source of calm and centering.

As you continue to breathe deeply and steadily, bring to mind the concept of your inner strength. This is the part of you that guides you toward making healthy choices, the part that empowers you to listen to your body and act with compassion and mindfulness.

Visualize this inner strength as a warm, glowing light within you. It may be located in your heart, your solar plexus, or any other area that feels right to you. See this light growing brighter and more radiant with each breath, filling your entire being with its

Now, gently bring to mind the goals you have set for yourself in making healthy food choices. Visualize yourself achieving these goals with ease and confidence. See yourself choosing nourishing foods, eating mindfully, and enjoying the process of nourishing your body.

As you visualize these moments, allow yourself to feel a deep sense of satisfaction and pride in your ability to make these choices. Know that every small step you take towards healthier habits is a testament to your inner strength and commitment to your well-being.

BETHANY ORRICK

In this state of relaxation and connection to your inner strength, repeat the following affirmations silently or out loud:

- I have the power to make healthy choices.
- I am mindful and present in my eating habits.
- I listen to my body and honor its needs.
- I am compassionate and kind to myself.
- I celebrate my progress and embrace my journey.

Take a moment to reflect on the journey you have embarked on. Feel gratitude for the awareness and understanding you have cultivated. Be thankful for the moments of mindfulness, the choices made with intention, and the compassion you have shown yourself.

Extend this gratitude outward, acknowledging the sources of your food, the people who support your journey, and the experiences that have brought you to this moment.

As we come to the end of this meditation, take a few more deep breaths, feeling the sense of calm and empowerment within you. Slowly bring your awareness back to the present moment, wiggling your fingers and toes, and gently opening your eyes when you're ready.

Carry this sense of inner strength, mindfulness, and self-compassion with you as you continue your journey towards making healthy food choices. Remember, you have the power within you to nourish your body, mind, and spirit.

Thank you for taking this time for yourself. May you continue to be guided by your inner strength and make choices that honor your well-being.

FINAL THOUGHTS

Awakened Eating is a lifelong journey that can transform your relationship with food and deepen your spiritual connection. By practicing mindfulness, reflection on your eating habits, and cultivating gratitude, you can enjoy a more fulfilling eating experience.

Bethany Orrick, an Emotional Intelligence Coach, began her healing journey seven years after the devastating loss of her 9-year-old daughter to brain cancer. Determined to transform her grief into a pathway for helping others, Bethany now specializes in using hypnosis to rewire the brain for success. She received her training at San Francisco State University and is certified by the National Guild of Hypnotists. Bethany's lifelong pursuit of emotional healing has led her to empower others on their journeys toward peace, fulfillment, and self-mastery.

Milton Keynes UK
Ingram Content Group UK Ltd.
UKHW042239011124
450424UK00001BA/83